A Way to Learn for Students

By

Jagdish Prasad Yadav

Copyright © 2023 Newbee Publication

ALL RIGHTS RESERVED

Thanks for Purchase

Scan QR code for more publications

This book may not be reproduced or transmitted in any form or by any means, electronic, mechanical, recording without written permission from the author.

Preface

Undeniably, academic qualification plays a significant role in our educational and professional lives. We all start our academic journey with primary school, the foundation for secondary education, eventually leading to university-level studies. For many of us, the university allows us to pursue a career and make something out of ourselves. However, for those fortunate enough to make it to university, it is essential that they put in their best effort for them to get the most out of their educational experience.

Education is a fundamental right and an essential part of life. It provides us with the tools and knowledge to succeed in life. The educational journey starts with primary school and continues to secondary school and, for the most fortunate, university. Through this journey, we gain the skills to make informed decisions on our future path.

Learning is an essential skill that everyone should have to succeed in life. It is one of a person's most important abilities, allowing them to think critically and understand new concepts. This is why I firmly believe that the learning process should be taught in schools as part of the curriculum, just like any other subject. By giving students the tools to develop their learning strategies and techniques, we can help them become more knowledgeable and independent learners. In addition, teaching them about learning can help prepare them for the future by equipping them with the necessary skills to excel in their chosen fields.

Learning is a crucial part of our evolution as human beings. We have developed the skills and knowledge to survive and thrive through learning. As we continue to learn and develop our skills, we have found new ways to solve problems, create opportunities, and build relationships with others. From mastering technological skills to creating innovative solutions, the art of learning has enabled us to stay ahead of the competition and remain relevant in today's ever-changing world.

Most college graduates' learning journey does not end after earning their degree. What they have learned in school or college serves as a foundation for the knowledge they gain. However, we do not always use the knowledge we gain in school or college for everything we do. It is strange but true that most college graduates do not even remember one course from their entire academic program when they look back at it ten years

Contents

1. INTRODUCTION..................................7
2. LEARNING......................................9
3. OWNERSHIP IN LEARNING..........................11
4. ASSOCIATION ABILITY............................15
5. CHUNKING......................................17
6. MEMORY..19
7. ELABORATIVE REHEARSAL..........................21
8. MAINTENANCE REHEARSAL..........................23
9. PASSION.......................................25
10. PERSEVERANCE..................................27
11. ACTIVE RETRIEVAL..............................29
12. SPACING.......................................31
13. INTERLEAVING PRACTICE.........................33
14. NAPPING BETWEEN STUDIES.......................35
15. COLLABORATIVE LEARNING........................37
16. DEBATE..40
17. DISCUSSION....................................42
18. DRAMATIC PLAY.................................44
19. EXPERIMENTAL LEARNING.........................44
20. INSTRUCTIONAL EFFECTIVENESS...................48
21. LECTURE METHOD................................51
22. PEER TEACHING.................................54
23. ROLE-PLAYING..................................56
24. PEG WORD MNEMONICS............................59
25. SLEEP...61
26. NOTES TAKING METHOD...........................63
27. MEMORY BOOSTING TECHNIQUES....................67

28. GRIT..69
29. EXPLICIT REMEMBERING............................71
30. INTERESTING APPLICATION OF LEARNING.......73
31. LOW STAKE QUIZZING....................................75
32. SPACING OUT PRACTICE..................................78
33. POSITIVITY IN THE SURROUNDING..................82
34. REFLECTION..85
35. SPACE VISUALIZATION....................................88
36. AUDITORY PROCESSING..................................90
37. ORIENTATION...92
38. ATTENTION SPAN..96
39. CONCEPT FORMATION....................................99
40. SOCIAL CONDUCT..100
41. INTERPERSONAL SKILLS................................103
42. SELF EXPRESSION..106
43. SELF CONTROL..108
44. SHARING/TURN TAKING.................................110
45. PROCRASTINATION..112
46. PLAY...114
47. POSTURE...116
48. REVISION..118
49. ORGANIZATION SKILLS..................................121
50. LEARNING STYLES...123
51. STUDY DURATION...127
52. CONCLUSION..130

INTRODUCTION

Welcome to "A Way to Learn for Students," a book designed to help students of all ages develop effective learning strategies and techniques that will enable them to succeed in their academic pursuits. Whether you are a high school student struggling to keep up with coursework, a college student looking to improve your grades, or a lifelong learner seeking new skills and knowledge, this book is for you.

Learning is a lifelong process, and it is essential for personal growth and development. However, many students struggle to learn effectively, despite their best efforts. They may find themselves overwhelmed by the material they need to know, unsure how to organize their time, or lacking the confidence and motivation necessary to succeed.

This book provides practical guidance and advice to help students overcome these obstacles and become more effective learners. We will explore various topics, from study habits and time management to memory techniques and problem-solving skills. Following the advice and strategies outlined in this book, you can approach your learning more confidently and achieve tremendous success.

Becoming a better learner may not always be easy, but it is always worthwhile. You can overcome any obstacle and achieve your goals with determination, hard work, and the right tools. Let's get started!

LEARNING

Learning is acquiring new knowledge or modifying and reinforcing existing knowledge, behaviors, skills, values, or preferences that can lead to a potential change in synthesizing information, depth of knowledge, attitude, or actions. Learning depends on previously acquired knowledge and can occur consciously or without conscious awareness. It is a lifelong process that can occur as part of education, personal development, schooling, or training and is facilitated by motivation. Learning may occur due to habituation, classical conditioning, or more complex activities such as play, and it produces changes in the organism that are relatively permanent. Ultimately, Learning occurs by changing the effectiveness of the synapses so that the influence of one neuron on the other changes.

Learning is a lifelong process that starts early in a living organism. In humans, learning involves changing the effectiveness of the synapses in the brain, which occurs when a neuron receives sufficient excitatory input. While the reference to prenatal education in the Indian Epic Mahabharata is likely an old legend, it is interesting to note that current neuroscience theories support learning to start at an early stage of life.

OWNERSHIP IN LEARNING

Yes, that's a great way to put it. Ownership in learning means taking responsibility and being accountable for your learning experience. It involves actively engaging in learning, setting goals, monitoring progress, seeking feedback, and making necessary adjustments. It also means recognizing that learning is a continuous process and taking ownership of personal and professional development.

When students take ownership of their learning, they become more motivated, engaged, and invested in the learning process. As a result, they are more likely to retain information, apply what they have learned, and pursue further learning opportunities. Additionally, taking ownership of one's learning can lead to greater confidence and self-efficacy, which can benefit both academic and non-academic settings.

Teachers and instructors play an essential role in fostering ownership of learning by providing opportunities for students to take ownership of their learning experience. This can include setting clear learning objectives, providing regular feedback, and encouraging self-reflection and self-assessment. It can also give students choices and opportunities to pursue their interests and passions within the learning environment.

In summary, ownership in learning is about taking control of one's learning experience, being responsible and accountable for one's knowledge, and actively engaging in the learning process. It is essential to effective learning and can significantly benefit academic and personal development.

Yes, John Dewey's ideas on student ownership and involvement in education are still influential today. He believed that education should be centred around the needs and interests of the students rather than just imparting knowledge to them. According to Dewey, students learn best when engaged in meaningful activities requiring them to think critically and make connections between their learning and their own experiences.

Dewey's emphasis on student ownership of learning has been incorporated into many modern educational theories and practices. For example, student-centred learning approaches such as project-based, problem-based, and inquiry-based learning encourage students to participate actively in their education by setting goals, identifying areas of interest, and working collaboratively with their peers.

By allowing students to take ownership of their learning, they become more invested in the process and are more likely to develop a lifelong love of learning. This, in turn, can lead to better academic outcomes and a more engaged and informed citizenry.

It is crucial to note that this sense of ownership and involvement is not limited to academic decisions but extends to the overall learning experience. For example, when students are given a say in the classroom, such as through classroom activities or group projects, they feel more invested in the learning process. It leads to better engagement, higher motivation, and better learning outcomes.

To achieve integration between student ownership and literacy needs, it is essential to establish open communication channels between students, parents, and teachers. This involves creating a safe and welcoming environment where students feel comfortable sharing their thoughts and ideas with peers and adults.

Furthermore, it is essential to provide students with the necessary tools and resources to succeed in their academic pursuits. This may involve providing additional support and guidance, such as tutoring or mentoring, or access to technology and other learning resources.

In summary, combining student ownership and literacy needs is crucial for meaningful student involvement and can lead to better learning outcomes. However, it requires a joint effort from different professionals, including parents, and necessitates creating a safe and welcoming environment, open communication channels, and providing students with the necessary tools and resources to succeed.

ASSOCIATION ABILITY

Yes, that is correct. Making associations between new and previously acquired information is a critical aspect of learning. This ability allows individuals to build on their existing knowledge and create new connections, leading to a deeper understanding of the material. Furthermore, associative learning plays a crucial role in forming long-term memories, which is essential for retaining information over an extended period.

Classical and operant conditioning are two types of associative learning that have been extensively studied. In classical conditioning, an association is made between a neutral and naturally occurring stimulus, resulting in a learned response. In operant conditioning, behaviours are reinforced through rewards or punishments, leading to a change in behavior over time.

Non-associative learning is another type of learning that involves a change in response to a stimulus without reinforcement.

Overall, the ability to make associations is a critical aspect of learning, and favourable conditions, such as adequate stimulation and opportunities for exploration, can foster this ability in children. Understanding the different learning types can also help develop effective teaching strategies and educational interventions.

CHUNKING

Chunking is a powerful tool for improving memory and learning new things more effectively. Organizing information into meaningful chunks can increase your capacity to remember and recall information. With practice and patience, you can become an expert at chunking and improve your ability to learn and retain new information.

To chunk information effectively, you can follow these steps:

1. Focus on the information: To chunk information, you must first pay attention to what you are trying to remember. This means actively engaging with the material and identifying the key points.

2. Understand basic/main ideas: Once you have identified the main ideas, you can start grouping related pieces of information together. Again, look for connections, themes, or patterns to help group the information into meaningful chunks.

3. Practice Chunking Examples: To get better at chunking, practice with examples. Try to find ways to group information that you encounter in your daily life. This could include creating acronyms, using mnemonics, or visualizing information in a particular way.

4. Rehearse and review: Once you have chunked the information, it's important to rehearse and review it. This means repeating the info multiple times until it becomes easier to remember. You can also try to recall the information from memory, which will help reinforce the chunks in your mind.

MEMORY

I'm sorry, but the idea that humans only use 3% of their brain or memory capacity is a common myth that neuroscientists debunked. While it is true that we do not always use all parts of our brain or all aspects of our memory, the idea of a fixed percentage of brain or memory usage is inaccurate.

The brain is highly adaptable and constantly changing based on experiences and learning. Unfortunately, our memories are also highly malleable and subject to distortions, forgetting, and reconstruction.

Moreover, the capacity of human memory is difficult to quantify, as it can vary widely based on individual factors such as age, genetics, and environmental factors. Therefore, assigning a specific percentage or number to memory capacity is impossible as it is highly complex and multifaceted.

While our memories are impressive and have vast potential, scientific evidence does not support using only a tiny percentage of our memory capacity.

ELABORATIVE REHEARSAL

Elaborative rehearsal is a cognitive strategy that involves actively engaging with new information to create meaningful connections between it and existing knowledge in long-term memory. When we encounter new information, it is initially stored in our short-term memory, which has a limited capacity and duration. However, by using elaborative rehearsal, we can transfer this information to our long-term memory, which can be more easily retrieved and used later.

One way to engage in elaborative rehearsal is to connect new information to existing knowledge and experiences. For example, suppose you are trying to learn about a unique historical event. In that case, you might relate it to a similar event you already know about or consider how it relates to current events or personal experiences. Making these connections creates more profound, meaningful associations more likely to be retained in long-term memory.

Elaborative rehearsal can also involve breaking down complex information into smaller, more manageable chunks. By organizing information into categories or creating visual representations, you can make it easier to understand and remember. Additionally, actively practising and applying new knowledge can help solidify it in memory.

Overall, elaborative rehearsal is a powerful tool for learning and memory retention. By actively engaging with new information and making meaningful connections to existing knowledge, we can improve our ability to understand and remember even the most challenging topics.

MAINTENANCE REHEARSAL

Maintenance rehearsal is a cognitive process where an individual repeatedly rehearses or thinks about a piece of information to retain it in their working memory or transfer it to their long-term memory. The repetition of information helps strengthen the neural connections associated with it, making it easier to recall.

In the context of children's learning, surrounding them with educational materials and providing them with consistent exposure to new concepts can be an effective way to facilitate maintenance rehearsal. For example, by surrounding a child with the letters of the alphabet, they will be consistently exposed to these letters and be allowed to rehearse and internalize them through repetition. Similarly, by providing children with consistent exposure to numbers, colours, and shapes, they can use maintenance rehearsal to learn and remember these concepts better.

However, it is essential to note that maintenance rehearsal alone may not be sufficient for more complex learning tasks. While repetition and consistent exposure can be effective for simple tasks such as memorizing letters and numbers, more complex tasks require more profound understanding and cognitive processing. Therefore, it is important to supplement maintenance rehearsal with other learning strategies, such as elaboration, organization, and visualization, to enhance understanding and retention of more complex concept

PASSION

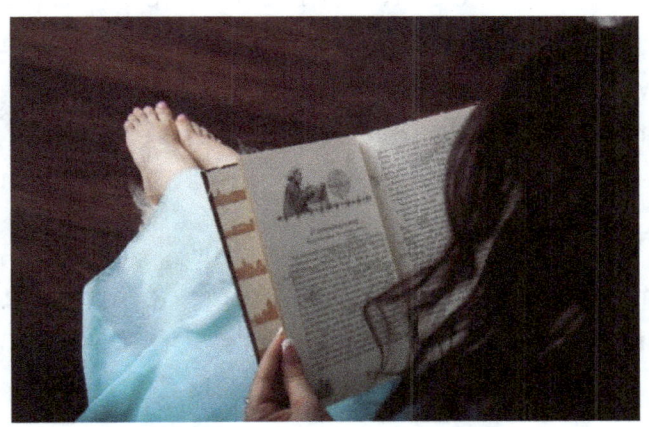

Passion is indeed a crucial factor in driving success in academic life. As you mentioned, developing a passion for learning is necessary to ensure continuous growth and improvement. Teachers play a significant role in fostering and nurturing students' passion for learning.

To create passion in studies, teachers must create an environment conducive to learning and enjoyable for students. By providing opportunities for collaborative reviews, encouraging creativity, and allowing time for play and fun, teachers can help students get into the flow of learning. In addition, keeping students' interests in mind, making emotional connections, and promoting innovation can inspire and engage students in their studies.

Furthermore, students should also strive to identify their passions and interests and align them with their academic pursuits. This alignment can help create a sense of purpose and motivation to drive their educational success.

In summary, passion is a vital component of successful learning. Teachers and students should work together to foster a love for learning and create an environment that promotes growth and development. With passion as the driving force, students can achieve their academic goals and succeed in their chosen fields.

PERSEVERANCE

Perseverance is indeed a crucial factor in achieving success in academic life. It involves persistence, effort, and the determination to keep going, even when things get tough. In addition, perseverance requires a mindset that embraces struggle and failure as opportunities to learn and grow. This mindset helps students to stay motivated and focused on their goals.

Creating a peaceful study environment, such as a library, can help students to stay focused and avoid distractions. In addition, it is essential to have a definiteness of purpose, a desire to learn, self-belief, determination, and a habit of working hard to persevere in their studies.

Perseverance is the game-changer in the long run and can separate average performers from geniuses. It is a critical element to succeed in difficult times, including learning. With perseverance, even the most challenging topics can be understood and mastered.

In conclusion, perseverance is a vital element in achieving academic success. Students can persevere and achieve their academic goals by developing a mindset that embraces struggle and failure as opportunities to learn, creating a peaceful study environment, and cultivating habits of hard work and self-belief.

ACTIVE RETRIEVAL

Active retrieval is a powerful learning technique that can help improve memory and enhance learning. By actively recalling information from memory, we are strengthening our brain's neural connections, making it easier to retrieve that information in the future.

Taking notes during active retrieval can also be very helpful, as it allows us to consolidate our learning and make it more concrete. By summarizing what we have learned in our own words, we engage with the material deeper and process it more meaningfully. These notes can then be used to create flashcards, an excellent tool for self-testing and reviewing information.

Active retrieval and note-taking are effective strategies for learning and retaining new information. By consciously engaging with the material, we can improve our ability to remember and apply what we have learned, leading to tremendous success in academic and professional pursuits.

SPACING

Spacing is a powerful technique for improving long-term memorization and learning. By spacing out our learning periods over a more extended period, we can consolidate learned information and improve our ability to retain it. In addition, interacting with the topics and enjoying the studying process is essential for better rewards.

One way to apply the spacing effect is to break up study sessions into smaller, spaced-out chunks rather than cram everything into a single, intense session. This allows the brain to consolidate information and create stronger neural connections, leading to better long-term knowledge retention.

It's also important to note that studying shouldn't be a chore. Choosing topics that align with our interests or current mood can make learning more enjoyable and engaging. This can help us stay motivated and focused throughout our study sessions, leading to better results.

In conclusion, the spacing effect improves our ability to learn and remember information. By spacing out our study sessions, interacting with the topics, and enjoying the process, we can achieve better long-term results and make learning a more enjoyable experience.

INTERLEAVING PRACTICE

Interleaving practice is a powerful learning technique that can help individuals improve their memory and retention of information. Rather than studying a single topic for an extended period, interleaving involves alternating between different topics or skills during a study session. For example, instead of spending an hour studying algebra, an individual might spend 20 minutes on algebra, 20 minutes on geometry, and 20 minutes on trigonometry.

The benefits of interleaving practice are numerous. One key advantage is that it forces the brain to constantly switch between different types of information, which can help build stronger neural connections and improve overall memory recall. Additionally, interleaving practice can help prevent the "forgetting curve," which occurs when new information is quickly forgotten after being learned.

Interleaving practice can be particularly effective when combined with spaced learning, another powerful learning technique. Spaced learning involves breaking up study sessions into smaller, more frequent sessions with breaks in between. By combining interleaving practice with spaced learning, individuals can optimize their learning and memory consolidation, improving their overall ability to retain and recall information.

Interleaving practice is a highly effective learning strategy that can help individuals improve their memory, retention, and ability to learn new skills and concepts. By incorporating interleaving practice and spaced learning into their study routines, individuals can optimize their knowledge and succeed tremendously in their academic and professional endeavours.

NAPPING BETWEEN STUDIES

Yes, that's correct! Napping has been shown to have various benefits for learning, memory consolidation, and cognitive performance. For example, even a short nap can help improve alertness, reaction time, and mood. In contrast, longer naps of 45 to 90 minutes can be especially effective for consolidating learned information and transferring it to long-term memory.

Napping has also been shown to improve frustration tolerance, emotion regulation, and associative memory and can be an effective alternative to caffeine for improving alertness and attention. In addition, recent research has suggested that a 10-minute power nap may be the most effective length for enhancing focus and productivity, with benefits lasting for up to 155 minutes after the nap. Overall, napping can be a valuable tool for anyone looking to improve their learning and cognitive abilities.

COLLABORATIVE LEARNING

Collaborative learning is an approach to learning in which individuals work together in groups or teams to achieve a common goal or to solve a problem. Cooperative learning promotes interaction, discussion, and knowledge-sharing among group members.

Collaborative learning can take many forms, such as group projects, discussions, debates, brainstorming sessions, and peer teaching. In these activities, learners are encouraged to collaborate, share their ideas and experiences, and learn from each other.

There are several benefits of collaborative learning, such as:

1. Enhanced learning outcomes: Collaborative learning allows learners to access broader knowledge and perspectives, leading to better learning outcomes.

2. Improved critical thinking skills: Collaborative learning encourages learners to think critically, analyze information, and evaluate ideas, which can enhance their necessary thinking skills.

3. Increased motivation: Collaborative learning can increase learners' motivation and engagement as they work together towards a common goal.

4. Development of social skills: Collaborative learning promotes the development of social skills, such as communication, teamwork, and leadership, which are essential in many aspects of life.

5. Preparation for the workplace: Collaborative learning prepares learners for the workplace.

Collaborative learning generally raises students' achievements, builds a positive relationship with peers, creates a learning community that values diversity, and promotes good knowledge and social skills.

Additionally, Collaborative learning promotes social and communication skills, which are essential for success in and outside the classroom. Therefore, collaborative learning can be a very effective teaching strategy for facilitating student learning and development.

DEBATE

Debating is a structured method of discussing and analyzing issues to persuade others to accept or believe your arguments on a particular topic. As a teaching tool, debates can help students to explore and understand alternative viewpoints, develop critical thinking and argumentation skills, improve communication and leadership skills, and conduct comprehensive research into a topic.

Research has shown that engaging in debates can have numerous educational benefits, including cognitive, presentational, and life-changing skills. Debaters can become better critical thinkers and communicators, improve their social interactions and become more understanding, improve their expression, and can be identified as leaders in practice. Moreover, debaters tend to become informed, active citizens who participate in improving society.

In conclusion, debates are an effective teaching tool that can benefit students in many ways. Students can widen their understanding of a topic by engaging in debates and identifying aspects they may not have initially seen. Furthermore, debates can help students develop skills critical for success in their academic and personal lives, such as critical thinking, communication, and leadership.

DISCUSSION

Discussion is essential to learning because it helps students process information rather than merely receive it. It makes a teacher's role a facilitator. Open-ended discussion promotes a collaborative exchange of ideas between a teacher and students. It encourages students to think, learn, problem-solving, understand or appreciate learning. The forum helps learners acquire knowledge, skills and attitudes rather than passive approaches focusing on lecture reading or viewing. It promotes learning both for teachers and students.

Discussion-based learning increases students' interest, and engagement in the topic and helps them to maintain focus. When asked to clarify their views, students understand different perspectives. Right questions and answers can get their students to think deeply and make better neuronal connections in the brain.

In addition to improving retention, discussion-based learning also helps to enhance critical thinking and problem-solving skills. When students engage in discussion, they are encouraged to analyze and evaluate information, consider different viewpoints and perspectives, and make connections between other ideas and concepts. When students are allowed to express their ideas and opinions, they feel heard and valued, which can lead to increased participation and engagement. It also creates a safe space for students to practice respectful and constructive communication, a valuable life skill.

Overall, discussion-based learning is an effective and engaging teaching method that can benefit teachers and students. By creating an environment that promotes active participation, critical thinking, and collaboration, teachers can help their students develop a deeper understanding of the course material, improve retention, and develop valuable life skills.

DRAMATIC PLAY

It's interesting to note that children who are good at acting out or mimicry may be potentially smarter and more mature than their peers. It could be because these children can use their imaginations and creativity more sophisticatedly and may better grasp abstract thinking and problem-solving.

TYPES OF PLAY

There are two types of play, which is structured and unstructured play:

- Structured play helps children integrate a focused mode of thinking. It helps them to learn problem-solving and collective decision-making.

- Unstructured play helps children to explore their inner subconscious brain and promotes a diffused mode of thinking and problem-solving. It also brings out the creativity of the child to the surface.

Benefits of Dramatic Play: -

1. Dramatic play teaches self-regulation

2. Encourages language development

3. Teaches conflict resolution

4. Supports literacy

5. Relieves emotional tension and is empowering to children

Dramatic play can help children develop essential skills and abilities, such as self-regulation, language development, conflict resolution, and literacy. It can also help them explore their creativity and imagination and provide a fun and empowering outlet for emotional tension.

Overall, incorporating dramatic play into the learning process can be a powerful way to engage and motivate children and to help them develop a range of essential skills and abilities.

EXPERIMENTAL LEARNING

Experiential learning is a highly effective teaching strategy that allows learners to actively engage with the material, develop new skills, and deepen their understanding through reflection and experimentation. The four models mentioned in the experiential learning process offer different perspectives and approaches to this type of education. Still, they all aim to promote hands-on learning and self-directed exploration.

One of the main benefits of experiential learning is that it helps students develop the competencies they need to succeed in life. By actively engaging with the material and experimenting with new ideas and skills, learners develop critical thinking, problem-solving, and decision-making skills that are highly valuable in a wide range of contexts.

Experiential learning also helps students achieve their goals by providing a clear path. Rather than simply memorizing facts and figures, learners are encouraged to set goals, experiment with different approaches, and reflect on their progress. This helps them achieve their academic objectives and gives them control and ownership over their learning process.

In addition, experiential learning teaches students how to guide themselves effectively through the learning process. By encouraging reflection and self-directed exploration, this type of education empowers learners to take ownership of their learning and become lifelong learners who can adapt to new challenges and opportunities as they arise.

Finally, experiential learning helps students understand how the lessons they learn in the classroom apply to real-life situations. By experimenting with different approaches and reflecting on their results, learners gain valuable insights into how their study concepts can be used in practical contexts. This enhances their understanding of the material and motivates them to continue exploring and learning more about the subject.

INSTRUCTIONAL EFFECTIVENESS

Educationalist & Mathematician Anant Kumar (Owner of Super 30) says, "Hard work, Proper guidance and Supervision are the secrets of success" in students' learning. He has shown his opinion beyond any reasonable doubt; hence it is essential to focus on Instructional effectiveness, which includes both Guidance & Supervision in Learning.

We can discuss a lot about the role of the Teacher, the Quality of Teaching, and the impact of practical teaching on the student's achievement. Beyond doubt, it is the teacher who lays the foundation of good learning." On a general note, the teachers or lecturers can positively develop or demotivate the learners from a particular subject. For students to learn effectively, the following must be in place:

1. Creating interest: One way to generate interest in a topic is to connect to the real world or students' experiences. For example, if teaching a math concept, an educator could relate it to a practical application like budgeting or cooking. Another approach is engaging learning methods such as hands-on activities, group work, or multimedia resources.

2. Instructor optimism: When instructors are optimistic about the subject matter, it can help motivate students and build their confidence. Instructors can convey their enthusiasm for the subject by sharing their experiences with it, highlighting its relevance to student's lives, and using positive language.

3. Introducing the topic: How a topic is introduced can set the tone for how students approach it. A good introduction can provide context and relevance, create curiosity, and generate interest. It is essential to use clear and concise language and avoid overwhelming

students with too much information at once.

4. Responding to queries: An essential aspect of instructional effectiveness is how instructors respond to student questions and feedback. A positive and respectful attitude can help create a safe learning environment where students feel comfortable asking questions and making mistakes. Instructors can also use questions to guide student thinking and help them develop problem-solving skills.

5. Rewarding effort: Recognizing and rewarding students' efforts can help motivate them to continue learning and striving for success. Rewards can take many forms, such as positive feedback, grades, certificates, or tangible incentives. Ensuring that rewards are fair and equitable for all students is vital.

In summary, instructional effectiveness depends on many factors, including teacher enthusiasm, engagement, and support for student learning. By considering these critical points, educators can help create a positive and effective learning environment that benefits all students.

LECTURE METHOD

The word 'lecture' originates from Latin. 'Lecture' translates roughly into "the act of reading." The term was first used to indicate verbal lectures in the 16th century. It was then used to depict the act of a lecturer standing in front of the students to impart knowledge. In recent times, the term now implies that the teaching method involves, first and foremost, a vocal performance given by a teacher to a group of scholars. Many addresses are conveyed by some pictorial aid, for example, slideshows, word text, an image, or a picture. Teachers may even use a whiteboard or chalkboard to emphasize essential points in their lecture, but a class does not require any of these things to qualify as a lecture. An influential person at the front of a class or gathering, delivering an educative discourse to a group of listeners, this can be called a lecturer."

Advantages:

1. Time-efficient: Lectures are an efficient way to deliver information to a large group of students.

2. Consistency: Lectures can ensure that all students receive the same information in the same way, helping to maintain consistency across the curriculum.

3. Expertise: Lectures are often given by experienced and knowledgeable educators who deeply understand the subject matter, which can benefit students new to the topic.

Disadvantages:

1. Passive learning: Lectures are typically one-way communication, with the lecturer delivering information and the students listening and taking notes. This can lead to a passive learning experience,

which may not be as engaging or practical for some students.

2. Limited interaction: Because lectures are typically delivered to large groups of students, there is often little opportunity for interaction between the lecturer and individual students, making it difficult for students to ask questions or get personalized feedback.

3. Retention: Students may have difficulty retaining information presented in lectures, mainly if the lecture is extended or the material is complex.

In conclusion, the lecture method can be an effective way to deliver information to students, but it is not without its limitations. Therefore, educators should consider their students' needs and learning styles when deciding whether to use the lecture method. They should also consider incorporating other teaching strategies like group work and hands-on activities to create a more engaging and practical learning experience.

PEER TEACHING

Peer teaching can also benefit students who hesitate to ask questions in a traditional classroom setting. When teaching their peers, they may feel more comfortable asking questions and seeking clarification from their peers rather than from a teacher or authority figure.

Additionally, peer teaching can help to foster a collaborative and supportive learning environment where students feel empowered to share their knowledge and learn from one another. This can be particularly valuable in subjects with many different ways to approach a problem or topic and where students can benefit from hearing multiple perspectives and approaches.

I agree that peer teaching can be a very effective learning method for many students. When students teach their peers, they reinforce their knowledge and understanding of the material and actively engage with the material in a way that can help them retain it better. In addition, when students are teaching their peers, they are actively engaging with the material and breaking it down into manageable pieces. This process helps solidify the information in their minds and can also help uncover any areas where they may have gaps in their understanding.

I believe peer teaching is a valuable tool for students to enhance their learning and understanding of a subject. However, it is essential to note that peer teaching should not be relied on as the sole learning method and should be used in conjunction with other teaching methods to provide a well-rounded and comprehensive learning experience.

ROLE-PLAYING

Role-playing is a highly effective teaching method that engages students in an interactive and immersive way. By assigning roles to the students, the learning process becomes more dynamic and personalized, allowing students to explore different perspectives and viewpoints related to the topic.

Through role-playing, students are encouraged to think critically and creatively, as they have to develop ideas and solutions on the spot. They also learn to communicate effectively, listen actively, and collaborate with their peers. These social and emotional skills are essential for students to develop, as they will help them navigate various social situations in the future.

Furthermore, role-playing can enhance students' language skills by allowing them to practice speaking and listening naturally. They learn to use appropriate vocabulary and grammar and improve their pronunciation and intonation as they interact with their peers and communicate their ideas.

Role-playing is an excellent way to make learning more engaging and memorable for students. It encourages creativity, imagination, and critical thinking while providing opportunities for social and emotional development and language enrichment.

Role-playing can be a very effective teaching tool for many different subjects and topics. By taking on different roles and engaging in different scenarios, students can gain a deeper understanding of the subject matter and learn how to apply it in real-world situations.

In addition to the benefits you mentioned, role-playing can help students build confidence and improve their public speaking skills. Students can practice and refine their communication and presentation skills in a safe and supportive environment by speaking and acting in front of their peers.

Furthermore, role-playing can also help students to develop empathy and understanding for others, as they are forced to see things from different perspectives and put themselves in other people's shoes. This can be particularly valuable for topics such as history, social studies, and literature, where understanding the perspectives and motivations of different characters is vital to gaining a deeper understanding of the subject matter.

Role-playing can be a powerful teaching tool that engages students in a way that traditional classroom instruction may not. By providing a fun, interactive, and immersive learning experience, role-playing can help students to develop a deeper understanding of the subject matter and the skills they need to apply it in the real world.

PEG WORD MNEMONICS

Mnemonics is also a tool for improving memory retention and recall, and peg word mnemonics are a specific type of mnemonic that use a sequence of rhyming words as a framework for memorization. It involves associating each item with a peg word that rhymes with a number and has a distinctive image or sound. The peg words themselves serve as "hooks" on which you can hang other pieces of information, making it easier to remember them in the correct order.

Here are some examples of peg word mnemonics:

One is a bun; two is a shoe; three is a tree; four is a door; five is a hive; six is sticks; seven is heaven; eight is a gate; nine is a vine; ten is a hen

You can use these peg words to remember a list of ten items by associating each item with its corresponding peg word. For example, in a grocery list that includes eggs, milk, bread, apples, and bananas, you could picture a bun with eggs on top, a shoe filled with milk, a tree made of bread, a door with apples growing on it, and a hive filled with bananas.

You can also use this peg word sequence to remember a list of ten items. Or, if you need to remember a list of historical events in chronological order, you could associate each event with its corresponding peg word. So, you might picture a bun with the signing of the Magna Carta, a shoe with the invention of the printing press, a tree with the founding of the United States, and so on.

Peg word mnemonics can be customized to suit your needs and can be a fun and effective way to improve your memory skills.

SLEEP

Sleep is indeed crucial for our overall health and well-being. Adequate sleep helps us recharge, repair, and rejuvenate our body and mind.

Establishing a good sleep routine is equally important to have an environment conducive to sleep. A cooler and dark room with a temperature lower than optimal is recommended. It is also advisable to avoid consuming beverages such as tea and coffee, which contain caffeine that can interfere with sleep. Consuming fatty foods, incredibly close to bedtime, should also be avoided.

In addition, it is essential to create a sleep-conducive environment by eliminating distractions such as media gadgets from the bedroom. The blue light emitted by electronic screens interferes with melatonin (a sleep hormone) production making it more difficult to fall asleep. Establishing a regular sleep schedule and sticking to it, even on weekends, can also be beneficial for getting a good night's sleep.

Establishing a good sleep routine is critical for our overall health and well-being.

Creating a cooler, dark, and quiet sleep environment can help promote better sleep. Avoiding caffeinated beverages, fatty foods, and electronic devices before bedtime can also help you sleep better. Additionally, following a regular sleep schedule and engaging in relaxation techniques before bed promotes better sleep.

It is worth noting that everyone's sleep needs can differ, and underlying medical conditions or lifestyle factors may affect sleep quality. Therefore, if you continue to experience sleep issues, it may be helpful to consult a healthcare provider or a sleep specialist for further evaluation and management.

NOTES TAKING METHOD

Students can employ note-taking methods to ensure they retain the information they learn. For example, the Cornell method divides the page into three sections: a main note-taking section, a cues section, and a summary section. The main note-taking area records the most important information from the lecture or reading material. At the same time, the cues section is used to write down questions or prompts that will help trigger memory recall when reviewing the notes. Finally, the summary section is used to jot down the lecture's main points or reading material in your own words.

Another effective note-taking method is the mind-mapping technique. Mind mapping involves visualising the main ideas and subtopics connected through lines and branches. This method benefits visual learners who prefer to see the relationships between concepts.

Regardless of the method chosen, it is essential to ensure that notes are concise and relevant to the topic. The notes should be written in a way that makes sense to the individual student, using their language and abbreviations if necessary. Reviewing the notes regularly is essential to help commit the information to memory. By incorporating effective note-taking techniques into their study routine, students can improve their retention of information and perform better in their studies.

Note-taking is an essential skill for students to develop as it helps to retain important information and recall it later. To make the most of your note-taking experience, following a few tips and techniques that suit your learning style is essential.

1. Be organized: Keep a separate notebook or a section for each subject or topic in your binder. Use headings, subheadings, bullet

points, and numbering to structure your notes and make them easy to read.

2. Listen actively: Pay attention to the speaker, and try to identify the main ideas, key concepts, and essential details. Focus on understanding the material rather than trying to write down everything. Use abbreviations and symbols to save time and space.

3. Use your own words: Write down the information in your own words, using simple language and sentence structure. Avoid copying word-for-word from the lecture or textbook. Paraphrasing and summarizing the material helps you to understand it better and remember it longer.

4. Review and revise: Regularly review your notes and edit them as needed. Add additional information, clarify unclear points, and cross out irrelevant or redundant material. Use highlighters or color-coding to emphasize important concepts.

5. Use technology: Consider using digital note-taking tools like Evernote, OneNote, or Google Keep. These apps allow you to

organize your notes, add images, audio recordings, and links, and easily share them with others. However, be aware of technology's potential distractions and ensure you are not getting side-tracked during class.

Effective note-taking requires active listening, critical thinking, and a willingness to engage with the material. With practice and perseverance, you can develop a note-taking style that works best for you and helps you succeed in your academicpursuits.TopofFormBottomofForm

MEMORY BOOSTING TECHNIQUES

Many effective memory-boosting techniques can help improve memory and brain plasticity. Here are a few methods that can be helpful:

1. Repetition: One of the most effective ways to remember information. Repeating information several times, either out loud or in writing, helps to reinforce it in your memory.

2. Mnemonics: Mnemonics are memory aids that use visual, auditory, or other sensory cues to help you remember information. For example, you are using an acronym to remember a list of items or creating a story to remember a sequence of events.

3. Association: Associating new information with something you already know can help you remember it more efficiently, for example, associating a person's name with their appearance or where you met them.

4. Visualization: Visualizing information can help you remember it better. For example,

imagine a picture or scene related to the information you want to remember.

5. Chunking: Breaking down information into smaller, more manageable chunks can help you remember it better. For example, grouping numbers or letters together into more minor sequences.

6. Sleep: Getting enough sleep is essential for memory consolidation. During sleep, your brain processes and consolidates new information into your long-term memory.

7. Exercise: Exercise has been shown to improve memory and brain function. Regular physical activity can help increase blood flow to the brain, improving cognitive function.

GRIT

Grit is a non-cognitive factor that plays a significant role in successful outcomes in various fields, including academic learning. It is related to consistency in the topic of interest and effort perseverance. Grit has weak to moderate associations with educational variables, with perseverance being a stronger predictor of academic performance. Grit is a mental strength resource, unique and essential to some cultures, including the Finnish culture. Empirical studies have scrutinized the factors that promote grit among students, examining whether students with a growth mindset and high obligation to their educational objectives tend to be gritty in academic learning. While the impact of grit on achievement was smaller than the effect of other factors, such as expectancies of success, ability, self-concept, or school engagement, determination had an immediate consequence. Grit plays a significant role in academic success and other fields, such as the military and the workplace. Grit is the combination of consistency in the topic of interest and effort perseverance, and it has been associated with positive educational outcomes, including higher CGPA and institutional achievements. However, research has shown that grit has a weak to moderate association with academic variables. Its impact on achievement is smaller than that of other factors, such as expectancies of success, ability, self-concept, or school engagement. To better understand the associations between grit and academic outcomes, recent studies have examined grit as having two-faced perspectives, with perseverance being a stronger predictor of academic performance than overall grit scores. While grit is essential in academic learning, it is not the only factor contributing to success. It should be viewed with other traits, such as self-efficacy and a growth mindset.

EXPLICIT REMEMBERING

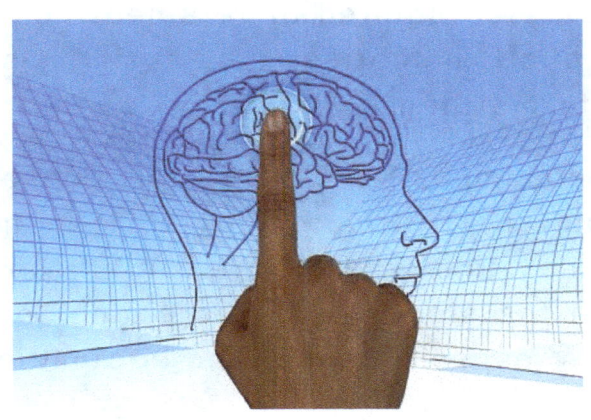

If students know the type of memory, they can train themselves to remember more effectively and efficiently. Remembering and memory can be divided into two main types: implicit and explicit.

Explicit memory involves conscious memories that we can intentionally recall and articulate, including personal experiences and memorized facts and information. Implicit memories, on the other hand, are memories that we acquire or retain more quickly and without conscious effort.

Remembering things is crucial for learning, and explicit memory is the most effective form.

Explicit memory involves conscious memories we can intentionally recall and articulate, such as personal experiences and memorizing facts and information. On the other hand, implicit memories are acquired or retained much faster than explicit memories, and a single stimulus usually forms them.

The hippocampus is crucial for consolidating data from short-term to long-term memory. At the same time, the prefrontal cortex is essential for storing and recreating long-term memories, especially facts and information.

Examples of different types of memories include self-composed, longitudinal, declarative, sequence, and semantic memories. Self-composed memories combine semantic and episodic memories, while longitudinal memories help us navigate the world around us. Declarative memory is the conscious thought of recalling information, while sequence memories involve placing personal experiences. Finally, semantic memories involve remembering data, descriptions, and notions.

Understanding the different types of memories can help individuals improve their ability to learn and remember information effectively.

INTERESTING APPLICATION OF LEARNING

Everyone is different, and they have a different style of learning & preferences. Therefore, there is no learning approach that can be one-size-fits-all to education. Consequently, it is essential to employ various active learning methods and strategies to cater to the diverse needs of learners. The techniques mentioned above, such as casting, deep reflection, hunting, joint virtual classrooms, social media messages, exemplary learning, and the riddling system, can make the learning process more engaging and interactive.

Moreover, it is crucial to keep up with technological advancements in education and incorporate them into the learning process. This way, learners can stay engaged and interested in the learning process, making it more effective.

In conclusion, teachers and learning professionals must be open-minded and creative in their approach to teaching to ensure that learners remain interested and engaged in the learning process. Furthermore, by adopting exciting and innovative methods, students develop a deeper understanding of the subject matter and apply it in real-life situations.

It is essential for learning professionals to keep up with the latest advances in technology and learning methods to stay relevant and effective in their roles. Whatever process works best for a particular teacher or student should be carefully evaluated and implemented.

Overall, active learning is a dynamic and exciting process that can improve comprehension, retention, and application of knowledge. By using innovative and creative strategies, educators can help their students achieve tremendous success and fulfilment in their academic and professional pursuits.

LOW STAKE QUIZZING

Low-stakes quizzing is a helpful tool for enhancing learning outcomes. It involves various ways, such as providing learners with multiple opportunities to demonstrate understanding, encouraging them to take ownership of their learning, directing them to the proper resources to fill potential learning gaps, and reducing anxiety associated with quizzes and exams. Meaningful feedback about finding the answer, a statement of the correct answer, and a detailed explanation of the solution can enhance learning outcomes by encouraging interaction with the content, filling any learning gaps, and inspiring mastery. It is essential to ensure that the tests are low-stakes, avoid unnecessary anxiety and stress, and focus on broader understanding rather than pass or fail assessment checks. Organized lists of knowledge and topic-based assessments can also help track whether pupils remember critical aspects of the topic taught and identify areas for expansion.

Overall, incorporating low-stakes quizzes in the learning process can provide several benefits for both learners and instructors. It offers multiple opportunities for learners to demonstrate their understanding and encourages them to take ownership of their learning. It also helps instructors identify potential learning gaps and direct learners to the appropriate resources to fill those gaps.

Meaningful feedback is a crucial component of low-stakes testing as it allows learners to interact with the content and fill any learning gaps independently. It also encourages mastery and reduces learner anxiety often associated with online quizzes and exams.

It is crucial to keep the test low-stakes to avoid creating unnecessary stress and anxiety for learners. Running topic-based assessments can provide a good comprehension of pupil/class strengths and areas for expansion. However, mixing up the actual evaluation can lead to misperception, primarily if knowledge is assessed within topic-based classifications.

In conclusion, low-stakes quizzing can be a valuable tool in the learning process, and when used effectively, it can enhance learning outcomes and student engagement.

SPACING OUT PRACTICE

Spacing out practice is an essential aspect of learning that involves spreading out repetition over time rather than relying on mass learning strategies. This approach has been shown to outperform the "fill up" strategy and has several benefits, including procedural learning, readying outcomes, and growing retrieval.

To effectively engage in the spaced practice, break down steps into manageable stages, use effective slide apps, encourage beginners to get involved, and model spaced repetition strategies. In addition, please encourage students to organize a study plan that reserves more sections or fractions of their time over a block, session, or year rather than cramming everything in at once.

Recognising that spaced practice may initially feel challenging and make students question their knowledge is essential. However, it is crucial to emphasize that sustained learning over time produces desirable results, especially when going into high-stakes situations.

Modern applications and technological aids can make spaced practice more accessible and easier to implement, particularly in prearranged structures and short timeframes.

Spacing out practice is an effective learning strategy that has numerous benefits. For example, students can use spaced repetition by applying specific policies and techniques, enhancing their learning outcomes, and preparing for high-stakes situations.

Spacing out practice is a crucial aspect of effective learning. The evidence suggests that spaced repetition outperforms mass learning or "fill up" strategies. Several mental functions are responsible for the advantages of spaced practice, such as procedural learning, readying outcomes, and growing retrieval.

Some policies need to be applied to engage in effective spaced practice. The process can be extended depending on the individual, and it is essential to enjoy the engagement. One easy betting tactic is to use social media trends like "Woman Crush Wednesday" or "Thank God It's Friday" to keep a broader array of content in play with pupils at any time.

Breaking down the steps into more manageable stages is also helpful.

It is essential to call pupils' attention to the fact that spaced practice will feel more challenging initially, but it is necessary for sustained learning. Therefore, it should be part of the equality in space try-outs. It is also crucial to encourage pupils to organize a study plan that reserves more sections or fractions of their time over the block, session, or year.

Modern applications can make spaced practice much easier for instructors, especially when driving learning toward schoolchildren in a prearranged structure and short timeframe. Unfortunately, the benefits of sustained learning are often not fully apparent until weeks, months, and years later. However, scheduled spaced practice over time will eventually produce desirable results that the student should notice going into high-stakes situations.

In summary, engaging in spaced practice is crucial for effective learning. Instructors should apply policies such as breaking down steps, designing effective slide apps, and using modern applications to make it easier. In addition, learners should be encouraged to organize a study plan that reserves more sections or fractions of their time and be made aware that spaced practice will feel more challenging initially. Still, the benefits will be noticeable in high-stakes situations.

POSITIVITY IN THE SURROUNDING

The learning environment plays a crucial role in students' academic output, and creating a positive environment can enhance their learning capabilities. The power of mental or emotional engagement can be harnessed to transform students' experiences and increase their capacity to bear the discomfort of working hard. To create a positive environment, it is essential to evaluate the current state of the educational setting and identify areas that need improvement. Strategies that infuse practice with progressive elements like hilarity, novelty, and interest can be implemented to improve the learning experience. These simple approaches can cushion the adverse effects of factors that threaten a positive classroom environment and help students evade getting caught in a negative spiral that can disrupt learning. Overall, creating a positive atmosphere in the classroom can yield lasting results and enhance students' learning and academic success.

A positive environment generates a positive vibe that makes students eager to learn, develop trust in their teacher and peers, tackle questions, and be part of the learning process. While many factors can threaten a positive classroom environment, we can adopt simple approaches to cushion their adverse effects and create the right solutions.

One approach to creating a positive environment is to harness the power of mental or emotional engagement. This can be achieved by integrating strategies that immunize students against negative feelings and experiences that can impact learning. In addition, these strategies should be easy to implement and yield lasting results, such as creating a classroom culture that values humour, novelty, and interest.

To create a positive learning environment, it is essential to evaluate the current state of the educational setting and identify areas that need improvement. Then, with a little effort, teachers can transform the experience of their students every day, leading to a more efficient and engaging learning experience. Ultimately, these efforts can increase students' capacity to bear the discomfort of working hard and accepting that critical, intelligent discernment and perseverance are the keys to excellent know ledge.

REFLECTION

Reflection is a process of thinking about and analyzing our experiences, actions, and thoughts. It involves examining what we have learned, how we have grown, and what we can do differently in the future. Reflective practices can help students better understand themselves, identify their strengths and weaknesses, and learn from their mistakes.

There are many ways in which students can engage in reflective practices. For example, they can write about their experiences in a journal or blog, discuss their thoughts and feelings with peers or mentors, or use guided prompts to reflect on specific learning experiences. By engaging in these practices, students become more self-aware, develop critical thinking skills, and become more effective learners.

The benefits of reflection extend beyond the classroom. Reflective practices can help students to develop essential life skills, such as goal-setting, problem-solving, and decision-making. In addition, reflecting on their experiences makes students more confident, resilient, and self-directed.

The relevance of reflection to teenage learning is significant. Adolescents are at a stage where they are exploring and developing their identity, and reflection can help them understand their strengths, weaknesses, values, and beliefs. In addition, by reflecting on their experiences, they can gain insights into their thought processes, emotions, and behaviours, leading to a deeper understanding of themselves.

Reflection can also help students become more self-directed learners. By regularly evaluating their learning strategies and outcomes, they can identify what works best for them and make adjustments as needed. This can lead to more effective learning and better academic performance.

Furthermore, reflection can help students develop critical thinking skills. By analyzing their experiences and identifying patterns and connections, they can learn to think more deeply and critically. This can also lead to increased creativity and problem-solving skills.

A reflection is a valuable tool for teenage learning as it promotes self-awareness, self-direction, critical thinking, and personal growth. Teachers and parents can encourage reflection by providing opportunities for students to reflect on their experiences, ask thought-provoking questions, and provide feedback on their reflective writing.

SPACE VISUALIZATION

Online resources and tools are available for individuals who want to improve their spatial visualization skills. These tools range from apps and video games that help you practice spatial reasoning to online courses and workshops that teach you techniques for improving your spatial visualization abilities.

In addition to these resources, there are also several exercises that you can do on your own to improve your spatial visualization skills. These exercises may involve mentally rotating objects, manipulating shapes in your mind, or imagining how different things might fit together.

It's important to remember that spatial visualization, like any skill, can be improved with practice and dedication. By actively working to improve your spatial visualization abilities, you can enhance your performance in a wide range of fields and activities, from art and design to engineering and construction.

Additionally, seeking out experiences that require spatial visualization can be beneficial, such as taking up a hobby like woodworking, sculpting, or rearranging furniture in your home. These activities and exercises can strengthen your spatial visualization abilities and improve your performance in related fields.

In conclusion, spatial visualization is essential in many professions and everyday activities. While some people may have a natural talent for it, it is a skill that can be developed and improved through practice and training. By improving your spatial visualization abilities, you can enhance your performance and creativity in various areas of life.

AUDITORY PROCESSING

Auditory processing plays a crucial role in learning, especially in language development, reading, and comprehension. Auditory processing refers to the ability of the brain to process and make sense of the sounds we hear. This includes the ability to differentiate between different sounds, recognize patterns in sounds, and understand spoken language.

When we learn new information, we often rely on our ability to hear and process auditory information. For example, when learning a new language, we must listen to and distinguish between different sounds and phonemes to correctly pronounce and understand words.

Similarly, when reading, we use our auditory processing abilities to recognize and understand the sounds of words, which helps us to comprehend the meaning of the written text.

In addition to language and reading, auditory processing is essential for learning in other areas, such as math and science. For example, students need to hear and process verbal explanations of equations and concepts to understand them when learning math concepts. Similarly, students must listen to and understand scientific reasons to grasp complex ideas and theories when studying science.

Overall, auditory processing plays a critical role in learning, and difficulties in this area can significantly impact a person's ability to learn and succeed academically.

ORIENTATION

These are great strategies for teachers to encourage students to learn and stay engaged. Here are some additional tips that may be helpful:

- Use technology to enhance learning. For example, incorporate multimedia presentations, videos, online quizzes, and other interactive tools to make the learning experience more engaging and dynamic.

- Foster a sense of community and collaboration in the classroom. Encourage students to work in groups, share ideas, and help each other learn.

- Use real-world examples and applications to illustrate the relevance of the subject matter. This can help students see the practical value of their learning and motivate them to apply it in their own lives.

- Create a positive and inclusive classroom environment. Respect and value diversity, encourage open dialogue, and establish clear expectations and boundaries for behaviour.

- Be flexible and adaptable in your teaching approach. Different students have different learning styles and preferences, so try to offer a variety of teaching methods and activities that cater to different needs.

- Encourage creativity and innovation. Allow students to explore their interests and passions within the framework of the subject matter and challenge them to think outside the box and develop their solutions and ideas.

- Emphasize the process of learning rather than just the result. Please encourage students to reflect on their

- Learning journey, identifying their strengths and weaknesses, and setting goals for improvement.

- Show enthusiasm and passion for the subject matter. Your energy and excitement can be contagious and inspire students to take a more profound interest in the material.

- Use humour and storytelling to make your classes more engaging and memorable.

- Incorporate real-world examples and case studies to help students see the practical applications of their learning.

- Provide opportunities for group work and collaboration, which can help students build social skills and learn from each other.

- Please encourage students to ask questions and provide opportunities to explore their interests within the lesson context.

- Be flexible and adaptable in your teaching approach, as every student learns differently.

- Provide regular opportunities for feedback and assessment, as this can help students see their progress and identify areas where they need to improve.

- Create a positive and inclusive classroom environment where every student feels valued and respected.

- Be open and transparent with your students, and encourage them to share their thoughts and ideas with you. This can help build trust and rapport between you and your students.

Incorporating these strategies help students stay engaged, motivated, and excited about learning.

ATTENTION SPAN

A student's attention span is crucial for their learning process. Hyperactivity and the learning environment can hinder proper attentiveness, affecting their grades. Teachers can plan classes and identify attention spans to help students learn more effectively.

Parents can also help develop their child's attention span by setting goals, playing concentration games, and practicing deep breathing. For students who struggle to pay attention, removing visual distractions, breaking up tasks into smaller intervals, allowing for active involvement, practicing attentive behaviour, and building IQ through games can all help improve focus.

As a tutor, it's essential to take steps to help enhance meditation for your students and reward those who can focus on their education despite distractions. It's important to note that developing a good attention span is vital for academic success and success in other areas of life. It can lead to better decision-making, increased productivity, and improved relationships.

Encouraging students to adopt good attention habits early on can have long-lasting benefits for their future. Additionally, it's important to remember that every student is unique and may require different strategies to improve their attention span

It's important to understand that attention span can vary based on individual differences and external factors, but many strategies can help promote focus and concentration. For example, encouraging goal-setting, engaging in activities that require concentration, providing opportunities for physical activity and breaks, and breaking down tasks into smaller intervals are all effective techniques for promoting attention and learning. Additionally, exercising the brain through IQ games can help build cognitive abilities and improve focus. With the right strategies and support, students can develop strong attention skills that will benefit them academically and in other areas.

CONCEPT FORMATION

Concept formation involves the development of an idea by categorizing data into broader views. Learning simple concepts with only one crucial feature is more effortless than complex ones with multiple components. Models and trial-and-error techniques are helpful for concept learning. Real-life examples have representative features, while artificial examples have defining characteristics. Students' understanding of concepts evolves and can include non-typical examples. To learn better, students should focus on forming concepts as it helps them become more familiar with the subject.

SOCIAL CONDUCT

Our social conduct goes a long way in determining how much we know. For example, children from a very early age are taught to be fair and kind to others regardless of their age and relationship with them. This is because they are likelier to display a positive attitude towards learning and be motivated to perform well. When teachers show empathy towards their students, it helps to build trust and establish a positive relationship. Empathy can also be taught by encouraging students to reflect on their own emotions and the emotions of others. This can be achieved through group discussions, role-playing, and creative writing exercises.

Respect for Diversity In today's diverse world, it is essential to promote respect for differences in culture, race, ethnicity, religion, and gender. This can be achieved by creating a safe and inclusive learning environment that encourages open discussions and the sharing of different perspectives. Teachers can also incorporate diverse materials and resources to expose students to different viewpoints and cultures.

When students learn to respect diversity, they are more likely to develop a broader perspective and be more accepting of others.

Collaboration and teamwork are essential for success in school and the workforce. Teachers can encourage collaboration by assigning group projects and activities that require students to work together towards a common goal. This can help to develop critical social skills such as communication, problem-solving, and leadership. Students learning to collaborate and work as a team are more likely to succeed academically and personally.

One effective way to instil empathy in children is through reflection. Reflection can help children understand and appreciate the feelings and perspectives of others and encourage them to act kindly towards others. For example, teachers can ask students to reflect on situations where they have shown empathy and kindness or imagine themselves in someone else's shoes. This helps students to develop empathy and understand the importance of being kind to others. Additionally, teachers and parents can model empathetic behaviour and encourage children to do the same.

Collaboration is another important aspect of social conduct in learning. Students who work together and collaborate with their peers are more likely to learn and retain information better. Teachers can assign group projects or encourage students to work in pairs or small groups. Collaboration helps students develop vital communication, problem-solving, and critical thinking skills, fostering a sense of community and belonging.

Respect is also a crucial component of social conduct in learning. Students who respect their peers, teachers, and the learning environment are likelier to succeed in school. Teachers can establish clear expectations for behaviour and enforce consequences when these expectations are not met. Additionally, teachers and parents can model respectful behaviour and encourage children to do the same. Respectful behaviour creates a positive learning environment where students feel valued and appreciated.

In conclusion, social conduct plays an essential role in learning. By promoting positive behaviours such as appreciation, empathy, collaboration, and respect, teachers can create a positive and supportive learning environment where students can thrive and reach their full potential.

INTERPERSONAL SKILLS

Interpersonal skills are crucial in learning because they are necessary for effective communication and collaboration. When learning, individuals often work in groups or teams, and good communication is essential to achieve common goals. Interpersonal skills help individuals to express their ideas and listen to others' viewpoints, facilitate discussions, and resolve conflicts.

In addition to helping learners build positive relationships with others, interpersonal skills can also help learners develop critical thinking and problem-solving skills. When learners engage in discussions and debates with others, they are exposed to different perspectives and ideas, which can broaden their understanding of a subject and help them develop a more nuanced understanding of complex issues.

Interpersonal skills also help individuals establish positive relationships with their peers, mentors, and instructors. By building solid connections, learners can access resources, receive feedback, and seek guidance, enhancing learning outcomes. In addition, interpersonal skills such as active listening, empathy, and respect can help learners build trust, establish credibility, and develop a sense of community within their learning environments.

Furthermore, interpersonal skills can also help learners develop leadership qualities essential for success in many areas of life. For example, influential leaders often possess excellent communication skills, the ability to inspire and motivate others, and the capacity to build and maintain strong relationships. By cultivating these skills, learners can develop their leadership potential, take on challenging roles, and make meaningful contributions to their organizations and communities.

In conclusion, interpersonal skills are critical for learning because they enable effective communication, collaboration, relationship building, and leadership development.

Individuals with strong interpersonal skills are more likely to succeed in their educational and professional pursuits and are better equipped to navigate the complexities of our interconnected world.

SELF EXPRESSION

Self-expression plays a crucial role in learning, allowing individuals to effectively communicate their thoughts, ideas, and emotions. By expressing ourselves, we clarify our understanding of a subject or concept and engage in a deeper level of learning through dialogue and feedback from others.

One way to improve self-expression is by speaking up and sharing our thoughts and opinions. Joininggroups or attending programs that encourage public speaking can help build confidence and improve communication skills. Writing is another excellent way to express ourselves and explore our thoughts and feelings. Journaling or writing creatively, we can better understand ourselves and our experiences.

When individuals express themselves, they share their unique perspectives, which can broaden their horizons and help them gain new insights into the subject they are studying. This, in turn, can lead to a better understanding of the subject and improved critical thinking skills.

Dance and movement are also powerful forms of self-expression that allow individuals to connect with their bodies and emotions. In addition, power posing or dancing can help reduce stress and boost confidence, leading to a more positive mindset and approach to learning.

Finally, building a clothing pattern or style that reflects our inner self can be another way of expressing ourselves. We can communicate our personality and values to the world by embracing our individuality and creating a unique style.

In conclusion, self-expression is essential for effective learning and personal growth. By practising different forms of self-expression, we can develop the confidence and skills needed to communicate our thoughts, ideas, and emotions clearly and effectively.

SELF CONTROL

Self-control plays a crucial role in learning and academic performance. It allows students to manage their behaviour, thoughts, and emotions to focus on their studies and achieve their educational goals. Students who lack self-control may struggle with managing their time, staying focused, and avoiding distractions, leading to poor academic performance. Here are some ways in which self-control can help in learning:

1. Time management: Self-control helps students manage their time effectively by prioritizing tasks, avoiding procrastination, and staying focused on the task at hand. Students can manage their time efficiently and achieve their academic goals with good self-control.

2. Focus and concentration: Self-control helps students stay focused and avoid distractions, which is crucial in learning. Students who lack self-control may find it challenging to concentrate and get easily

distracted, leading to poor academic performance.

3. Delayed gratification: Self-control helps students delay gratification and resist the temptation to engage in immediate pleasures or distractions, such as playing games or watching TV. By delaying gratification, students can focus on their studies, which can yield positive academic results.

4. Emotional regulation: Self-control helps students regulate their emotions and avoid impulsive behaviour, which can lead to negative consequences. Students who lack self-control may struggle to manage their feelings and engage in disruptive behaviour, leading to poor academic performance.

In conclusion, self-control is a crucial factor in learning and academic performance. By practising self-control, students can manage their time, stay focused, delay gratification, and regulate their emotions, leading to positive educational outcomes. Therefore, developing self-control skills is essential for students to achieve academic success.

SHARING/TURN TAKING

Sharing and turn-taking are essential in learning, particularly informal and casual conversations. These skills enable individuals to participate in group discussions, share their ideas and perspectives, and engage in collaborative problem-solving. In addition, when individuals take turns speaking, they develop active listening skills, learn to respect other people's views, and contribute to a constructive learning environment.

Turn-taking skills are fundamental in informal conversations without a set task or agenda. In such situations, individuals must recognize when it is their turn to speak, listen actively to others, and build on what has been said. These skills can be developed through practice and rehearsal in similar settings, such as small group discussions, debates, or peer-to-peer tutoring.

To foster and develop turn-taking and sharing skills in learners, educators must create a conducive learning environment that emphasizes these skills. This may involve activities that encourage active listening, role-playing, group discussions, and other collaborative learning activities. In addition, providing learners with constructive feedback and coaching is essential to help them refine their turn-taking and sharing skills.

The importance of turn-taking and sharing in learning cannot be overstated. These skills enable individuals to engage in collaborative learning, share their ideas and perspectives, and contribute to a constructive and supportive learning environment. By providing opportunities for individuals to practice and develop these skills, educators and trainers can help to create more effective and engaging learning experiences for their learners.

PROCRASTINATION

Procrastination can have a significant negative impact on the learning capability of a student. When a student procrastinates, they delay the learning process and miss opportunities to study and practice, which can ultimately result in poor academic performance.

One of the primary effects of procrastination on learning is that it can lead to increased stress and anxiety. In addition, procrastination often causes students to leave their work until the last minute, resulting in rushing to complete assignments and feeling overwhelmed. This can lead to decreased motivation and a lack of focus, ultimately harming the learning process.

Procrastination can also cause a student to miss significant learning and growth opportunities. For example, when students delay studying, they miss opportunities to reinforce their understanding of the material and practice essential skills. This can ultimately result in a lack of mastery and poor academic performance.

Furthermore, procrastination can also harm a student's overall academic success. When students procrastinate, they may miss important deadlines or fail to complete assignments, leading to a lower overall grade. This can negatively impact a student's future opportunities for academic advancements, such as acceptance to a particular university or program.

In conclusion, procrastination can have a detrimental effect on learning. To avoid the negative impact of procrastination, students should work to develop good study habits and time management skills, and they should strive to complete their work in a timely and efficient manner.

PLAY

The role of play in learning is essential for both children and adults. Sport helps to stimulate the mind, boost creativity, and develop social and collaborative skills. In addition, it allows individuals to relax, relieve stress, and connect with others, which can contribute to overall well-being. Playful activities that test the brain can also improve cognitive function, memory, and brain tasks.

Play is a natural and enjoyable way of learning, and it stimulates the mind, enhances creativity, and boosts problem-solving skills. In addition, through play, children and adults develop social and collaborative skills, which help build positive relationships and create a sense of trust and cooperation. Play also helps reduce stress and improve well-being, vital for mental and physical health.

In conclusion, the benefits of play cannot be overstated. It is an essential aspect of learning and should be encouraged in children and adults alike. Parents, educators, and guardians should provide ample play opportunities and create an environment that promotes fun, creativity, and socialization. By doing so, individuals can learn effectively, reduce stress, and improve their overall well-being.

POSTURE

Posture is crucial in learning as it can impact students' physical and mental health and ability to concentrate and learn effectively. For example, poor posture can lead to various health problems, such as back and neck pain, eye strain, and fatigue, which can interfere with students' ability to stay focused and engaged in their studies. On the other hand, good posture can enhance blood circulation, breathing, and mental alertness, leading to better academic performance.

When a student is sitting with good posture, they are more likely to be alert and engaged in their work. In addition, they can breathe more deeply and fully, which can help provide more oxygen to the brain and improve cognitive function. Good posture also allows for proper body alignment, reducing strain on muscles and joints and preventing injury.

In addition to physical health benefits, good posture can also impact students' emotional well-being. A study published in Health Psychology Open found that adopting an upright posture can boost self-esteem, increase positive mood, and reduce negative attitude. This indicates that maintaining good posture can contribute to students' emotional resilience and help them handle stress and challenging academic tasks better.

Teachers and parents can encourage good posture in students by teaching them proper posture habits and providing ergonomic furniture and equipment. They can also remind students to take breaks, stretch, and move around frequently, especially during long study sessions. Additionally, incorporating activities such as yoga, Pilates, or other exercises that promote good posture can help students develop healthy habits and enhance their overall well-being.

In conclusion, good posture is vital for students' health, learning, and emotional well-being. By maintaining proper posture, students can enhance their focus, concentration, and academic performance while reducing the risk of physical and emotional problems.

REVISION

Revision is a necessary process in academic writing that involves critically reviewing and rethinking your paper to improve its quality. The term "revision" means to see again and approach the essay from a fresh perspective. This ongoing process involves reconsidering your arguments, reviewing your evidence, refining your purpose, reorganizing your presentation, and revitalizing your writing style.

You can use creative techniques to help you understand and remember the information when revising. For example, using images can be helpful, even if they are not professionally done if they make sense to you.

Revision is a well-known but often overlooked formula for exam success. It may seem daunting to students, as it requires analysing and revisiting all the material covered throughout the year. However, a systematic revision can help solve this problem and ensure exam success.

When studying and revising, practising relearning and recalling knowledge is essential. Research suggests that students should try to remember their abilities and then fill in any gaps in their understanding by relearning.

Revising improves the quality of your writing and helps you reflect on what you have written. In addition, it is an opportunity to learn about the craft of writing, which is closely tied to critical reading. To revise a piece conceptually, students must reflect on whether their message aligns with their writing goal.

Revising often demonstrates learning, as students' ideas and assumptions may change as they learn more from course materials, life experiences, and external sources. Large-scale changes to your ideas indicate that you have learned something you did not know before.

Stepping back and looking at your paper is essential to the revision process. This approach allows you to assess whether you effectively convey your intended message and how you can make your writing more engaging, concise, and clear.

Revision is a vital tool that enables students to reinforce and embed their learning, identify areas of weakness, and connect with other study areas. It is also an opportunity to practice applying knowledge and skills under exam conditions, preparing students for terminal exams.

ORGANIZATION SKILLS

Good organizational skills can significantly impact a learner's ability to learn and succeed academically. Here are some ways that organizational skills can affect learning:

1. Improved Time Management: Time management is a crucial aspect of organizational skills. By effectively managing their time, students can prioritize their tasks and work efficiently, completing their work on time. This helps reduce stress and anxiety, allowing students to focus on their studies and retain information better.

2. Better Planning and Execution: Organizational skills also help students systematically plan their tasks and projects. By breaking down complex projects into smaller, more manageable steps, they can execute them more efficiently. This enables them to complete their work with a higher level of accuracy, ensuring better learning outcomes.

3. Increased Productivity: Students who are organized can work smarter, not harder. They can better prioritize tasks and focus on the most important ones first. This leads to increased productivity, allowing them to accomplish more in less time.

4. Reduced Procrastination: Procrastination is a significant barrier to effective learning. Students with strong organizational skills can better plan and manage their time, reducing the likelihood of putting off tasks until the last minute.

5. Improved Focus and Concentration: Students who have a clear plan and defined strategies are less likely to get distracted or waste time. This helps them to stay focused and concentrate better on their studies, leading to improved learning outcomes.

In summary, good organizational skills are essential to learning effectively. By mastering time management, planning and execution, productivity, reduced procrastination, and improved focus, students can unlock their full potential and succeed in their academic pursuits.

LEARNING STYLES

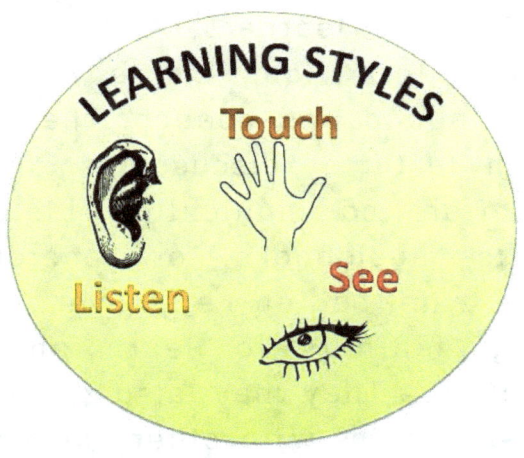

How you learn significantly impacts your overall learning because it influences how you understand and retain information. Therefore, identifying and utilizing your preferred learning style can enhance your learning experience and achieve better results. Here are some ways in which different learning styles impact overall learning:

1. Pictorial learners: Visual learners tend to absorb information better when presented in pictures, diagrams, or videos. They are good at recalling information they have seen before, so they benefit from visual aids and mind maps. Using images to

represent concepts, pictorial learners can better understand and remember complex topics more quickly.

2. Aural/Auditory learners: Auditory learners absorb information more effectively through sound and speech. They tend to excel in lectures, discussions, and other forms of oral communication. Listening to podcasts, audiobooks, or recordings of classes can be an effective way for auditory learners to learn and retain information. They may also benefit from discussing topics with others or explaining concepts to someone else.

3. Physical learners (Kinaesthetic): Kinaesthetic learners are hands-on learners who learn best through physical activities and experiments. They learn by doing and benefit from opportunities to manipulate objects or conduct experiments. Hands-on activities, role-playing, and simulations are all effective ways for kinaesthetic learners to learn and retain information.

Understanding your learning style can help you tailor your study techniques to suit your strengths. For example, if you are a visual learner, you might create mind maps or use flashcards with pictures to help you remember information. If you are an auditory learner, you might listen to recorded lectures or repeat information aloud to help you retain it. And if you are a kinaesthetic learner, you might try hands-on activities or create physical models to help you understand complex concepts.

Learning style can impact overall learning in many ways, as individuals tend to prefer to process information and retain knowledge. Here are some of the ways that learning styles can impact general education:

1. Learning Efficiency: When learners are exposed to teaching methods that align with their learning style, they learn faster and more efficiently. For example, a visual learner may benefit from seeing diagrams or videos, while an auditory learner may benefit from hearing explanations and discussions.

2. Engagement: Learning in a way that is engaging and enjoyable can increase motivation and overall learning outcomes. If learners enjoy the learning process, they are more likely to engage with and retain the material.

3. Retention: Matching teaching methods with learning styles can also improve the retention of information. For example, kinaesthetic learners may benefit from hands-on activities that allow them to apply concepts practically.

4. Frustration: If learners are forced to learn in a way that doesn't match their learning style, they may become frustrated and disengaged. This can lead to poor learning outcomes and even hostile attitudes towards learning.

Understanding your learning style can help you identify what works best for you and improve your learning outcomes. It's essential for teachers also to recognize different learning styles in their students and provide a variety of teaching methods to accommodate all learners.

STUDY DURATION

There is no single" one-size-fits-all "approach when deciding the duration of the study. What is a good study duration for effective learning, as the ideal study duration can vary depending on a variety of factors, such as the individual's learning style, the complexity of the material, and the individual's prior knowledge of the subject.

However, it is generally recommended that students aim to study for at least 2-3 hours per day for effective learning. This duration can be divided into shorter study sessions of around 30-45 minutes with short breaks to avoid burnout and maintain focus.

It's important to note that the quality of the study time is just as important as the quantity. Therefore, it's essential to use the time effectively and efficiently by prioritizing tasks, focusing on the crucial material, and engaging in active learning strategies.

Ultimately, the most effective study duration will vary from person to person, and it's essential to experiment with different study durations and techniques to find what works best for you.

The impact of study duration on learning is significant. The more time you spend studying, the more you will likely understand the content and develop a more profound knowledge of the subject. However, it is essential to note that the quality of the time you spend studying is just as important as the quantity. It is not enough to spend long hours studying if you are not using that time effectively and efficiently.

Good study duration skills involve prioritising tasks and focusing on what is essential. This means distinguishing between urgent tasks that must be done immediately and important tasks that can wait. By focusing on what is necessary, you can avoid getting distracted by less important tasks and use your time more productively.

Another essential aspect of good study duration is finding ways to make studying more enjoyable and engaging. For example, studying with peers can make learning more fun and interactive. By enjoying what you are studying, you are more likely to retain the information and develop a deeper understanding of the subject.

In conclusion, good study duration is essential for effective learning. By prioritizing tasks, focusing on what is necessary, and finding ways to make studying more enjoyable, you can use your time more effectively and achieve better results.

CONCLUSION

Adopting effective learning strategies to improve learning is essential, which can be done by having a willing heart and dedicating oneself to the learning process. Some ways to enhance learning include identifying different learning components, using them to one's benefit, and experimenting with different learning styles and methods. Additionally, it is essential to engage in active learning, such as asking questions, summarizing information, and teaching others. Finally, education is a lifelong process, and it is essential to improve one's learning skills to succeed in life continually.

Here are some tips for improving learning, retention, and retrieval of learned material:

1. Practice active learning: Active learning involves engaging with the material meaningfully, such as by asking questions, summarizing key points, or making connections to real-life situations. This can help you understand the material more deeply and retain it better.

2. Use multiple senses: Try to engage as many senses as possible in your learning process, such as by reading, listening, and writing. This can help to reinforce the material and make it easier to remember.

3. Break up your studying into manageable chunks: Instead of cramming all of your studying into one long session, break it up into smaller chunks over a more extended period. This can help you avoid burnout and improve retention.

4. Use active recall techniques: Active recall involves retrieving information from memory rather than simply re-reading or re-watching the material. This can help to strengthen your memory of the material.

5. Get enough sleep: Sleep is crucial for consolidating memories, so make sure to get enough sleep before and after studying.

6. Practice spaced repetition involves revisiting material at increasingly longer intervals over time. This can help to reinforce your memory of the material and improve retrieval.

7. Make connections to real-life situations: Try to relate the material you're learning to real-life situations, as this can help you better understand and remember them.

8. Test yourself: Self-testing can help you identify areas where you need to focus your studying, and it can also help to reinforce your memory of the material. Try creating flashcards or taking practice tests to test your knowledge.

Incorporating these strategies into your studying routine can improve your learning, retention, and retrieval of learned material.

"Thank you for choosing to read our book! If you enjoyed it, we would be grateful if you could take a moment to leave a review on Amazon or Google to help others discover the book as well."

For more Publication visit our site

www.newbeepublication.com

or

Contact us

newbeepublication@gmail.com

www.ingramcontent.com/pod-product-compliance
Lightning Source LLC
Chambersburg PA
CBHW072058110526
44590CB00018B/3228